Mitsumasa Anno

ANNO'S MATH GAMES IIII

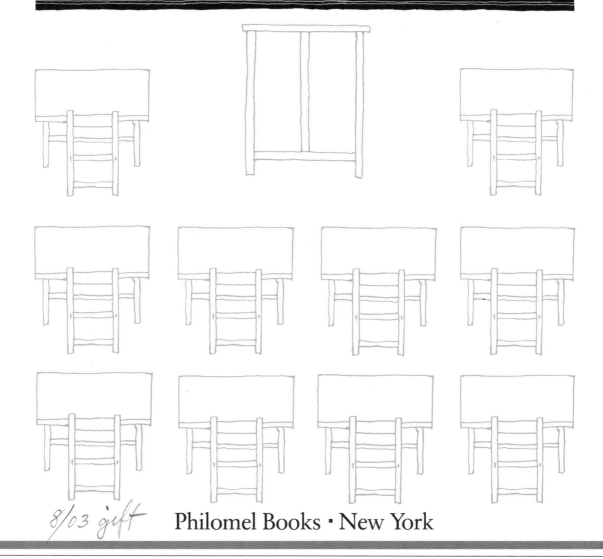

Philomel Books · New York

▪1▪

Changing Shapes with Magic Liquid

Our little friend is making a special magic liquid. He is making one liquid that stretches or shrinks things from top to bottom, and another that stretches or shrinks things from side to side. What do you suppose will happen when he mixes the two liquids and brushes it onto things?

Kross painted a face on his tummy, and Kriss is brushing the magic liquid onto Kross' tummy. You can see what kinds of things happen to his tummy as a result.

When the magic length liquid and
the magic width liquid are evenly
mixed together and brushed on
this donkey, he just gets bigger all
around without changing his shape.

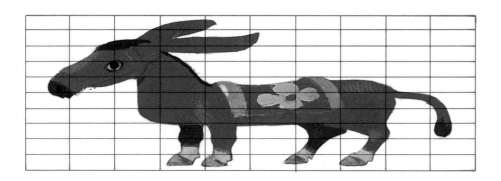

Look at the donkey when only the width liquid is put on. And look when only the length liquid is put on.

Now look what happens to this poor rabbit
when the liquids are not evenly mixed.

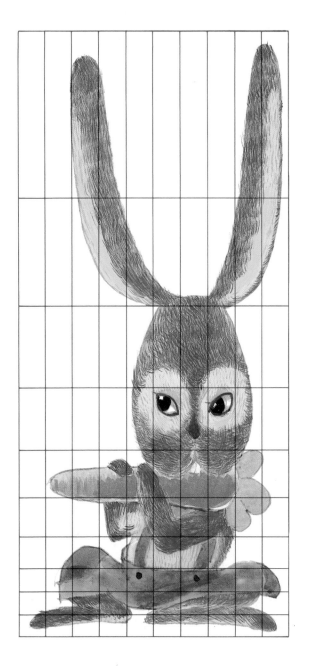
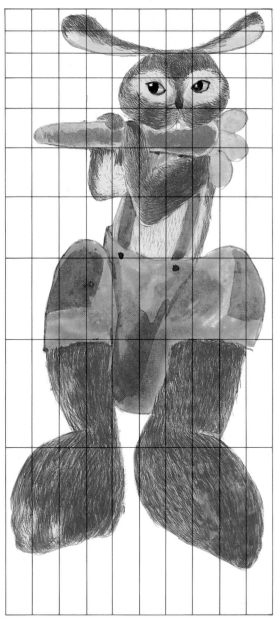

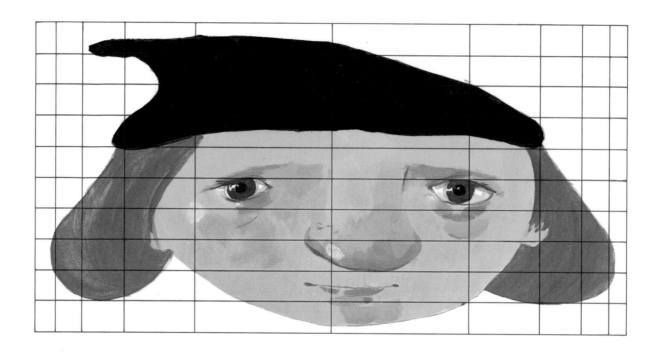

How do you suppose the liquids were
mixed here? Kriss' face has changed
in some funny ways.
Have you ever seen your own face changed like
this in a curved mirror at a carnival?

Look at Kross' face. It's changed too.
Try seeing how your own face looks
in a shiny spoon or a coffee pot or some
other curved reflecting surface.

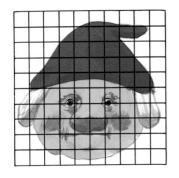

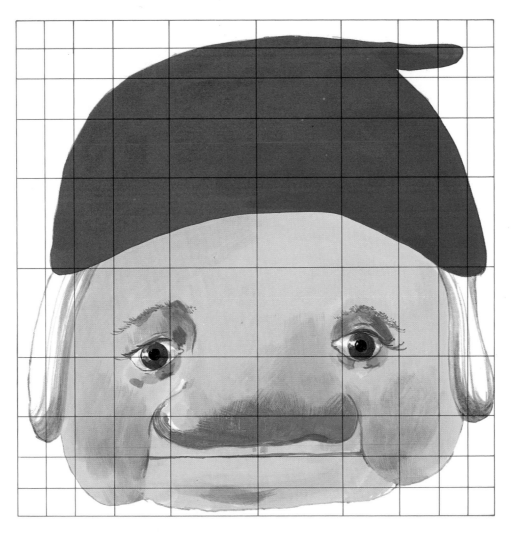

The liquid has changed the shape of this monkey in some strange ways. But notice that he still has the same number of arms and legs and that his eyes and nose stay above his mouth.

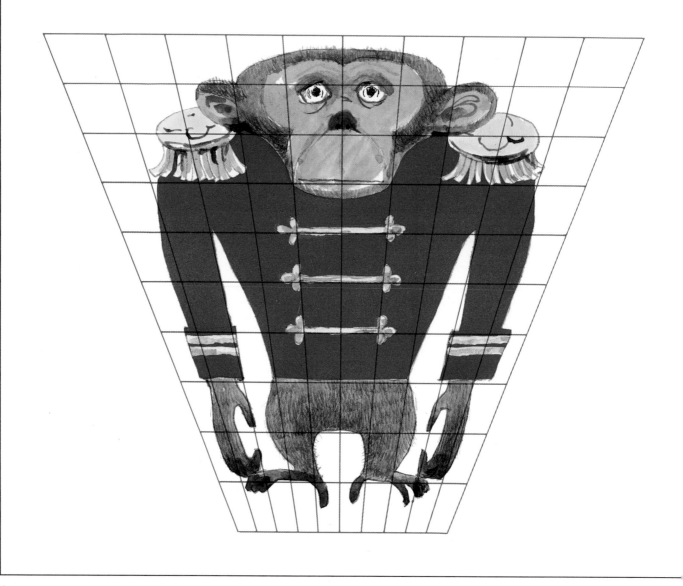

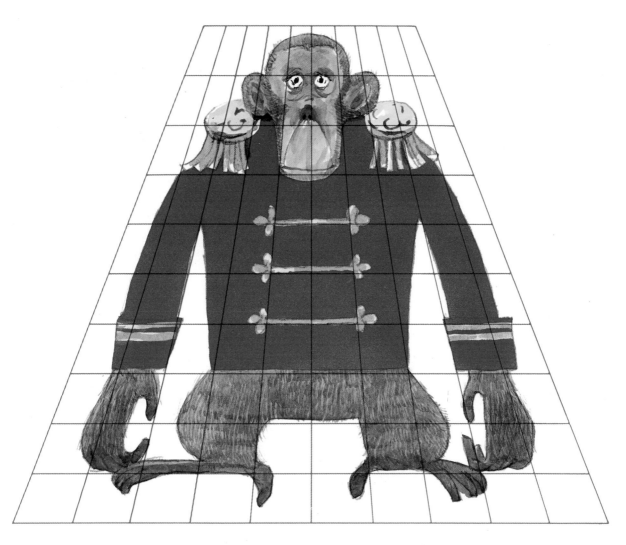

If you drew a picture on a big building and then looked at it from the side, it would look like this. The part of the drawing closest to you would look bigger than the part farthest away.

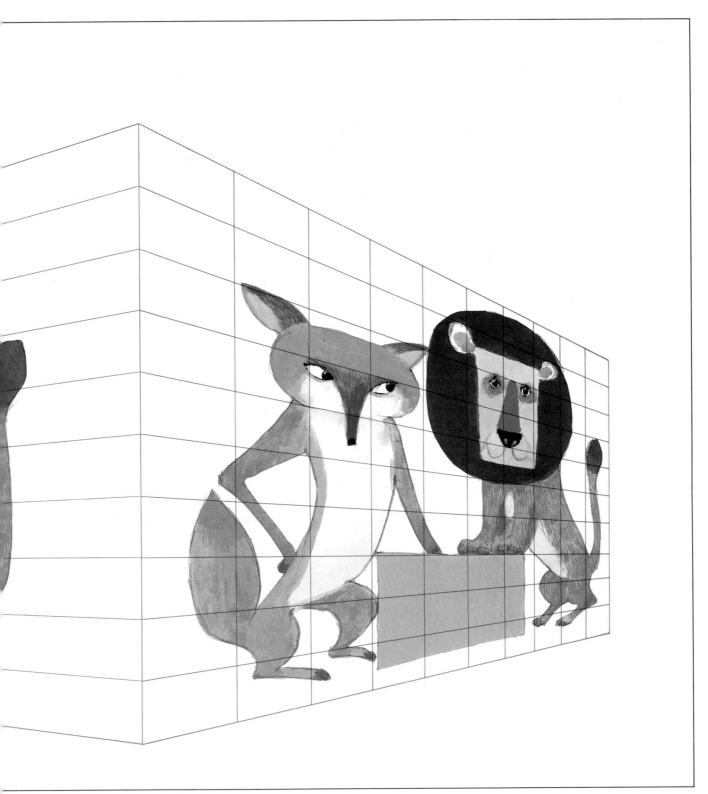

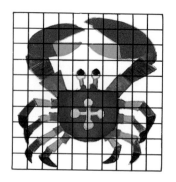

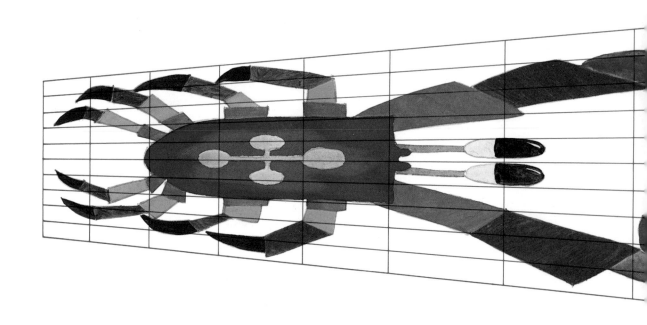

Hold the book out flat and slowly raise it to eye level so
that you are looking at the crab from the left side as our
little friend is doing. Do you see that the crab gets
smaller and smaller the closer to eye level it gets?
But again, no matter how much the entire shape stretches
or shrinks, notice the crab still has the same number of
eyes, a nose, and a mouth, and they are still
in the same places.

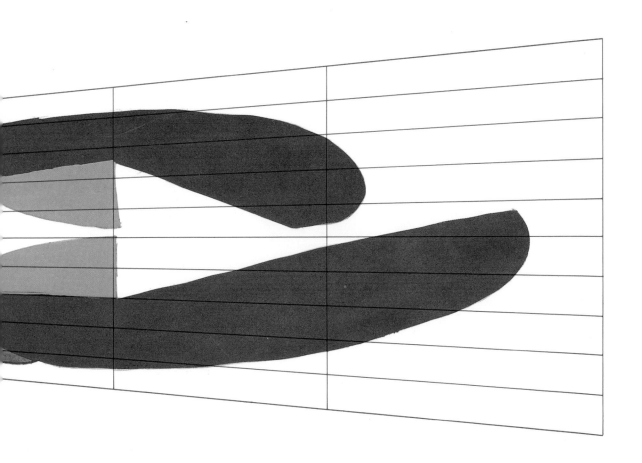

Kross is busy again with a new magic liquid. When he puts it on this piece of string, it can be stretched out like rubber. And stretched and stretched.

Look at this picture. Using the ⊘ shape of a circle with a line in it, examine carefully how a glove is being made.

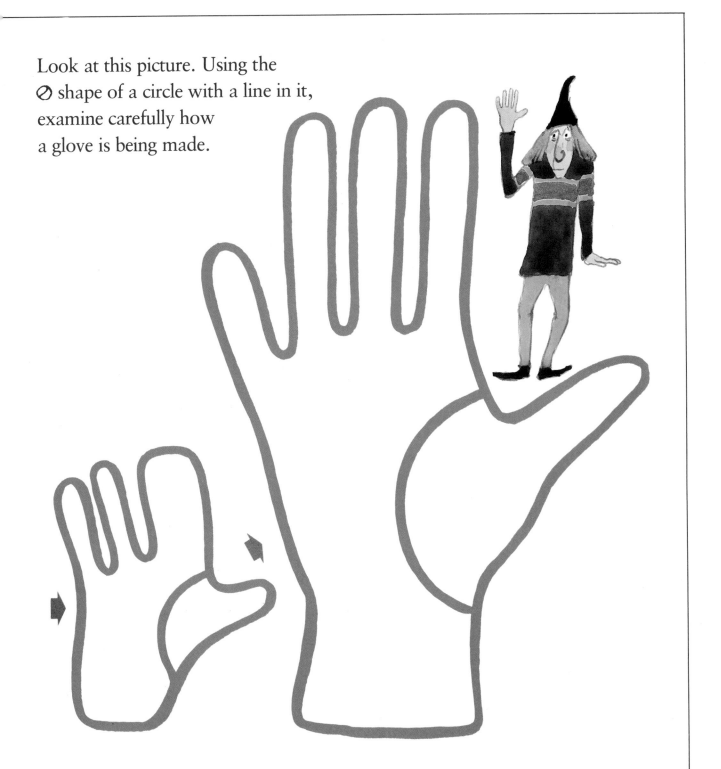

These different shapes can be sorted into two groups: things that were made from stretching and molding

⊘ a circle with one line in it, and

⊘ things that were made from stretching and molding a circle with two lines in it. Look carefully and sort them for yourself.

▪2▪

Exploring Triangles

When Kriss and Kross put together three squares of colored paper, it made one triangle in the center like this. Then they drew two new triangles. If you look carefully, you can find all three of the different triangles in their design at the bottom.

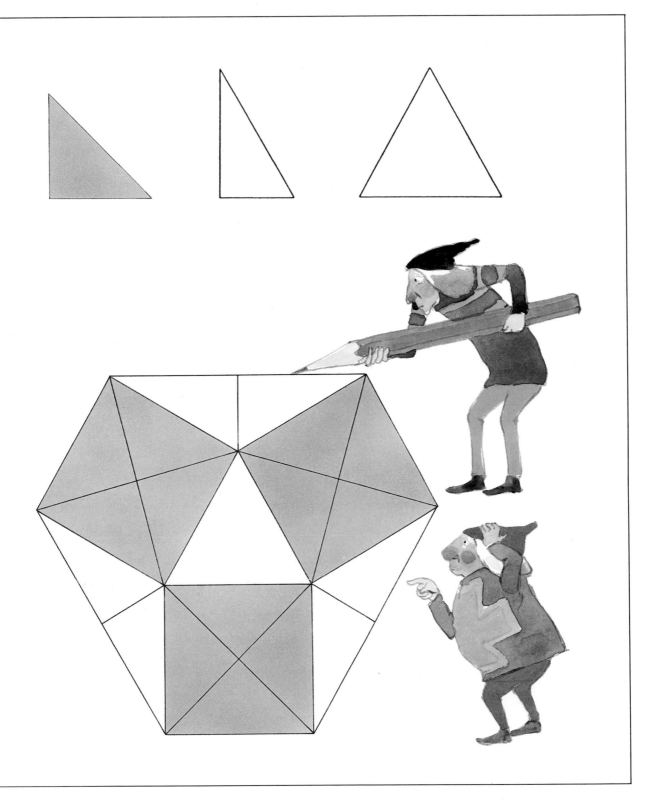

Kriss and Kross have discovered all
different kinds of shapes. Can you decide
which are triangles and which aren't?

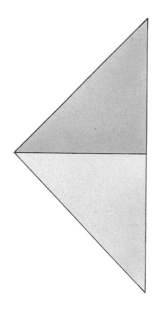
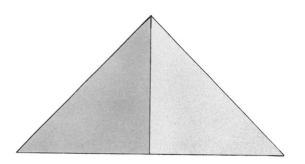
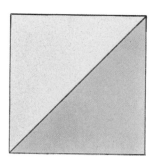

If we put together two triangles that have the same shape, we can make a new shape. Our little friends made these shapes by putting together two each of the three different triangles on page 29. What kind of new shapes did they make?

Kross and Kriss got lots more triangles and put them all together! Do you see the triangles in the design below?

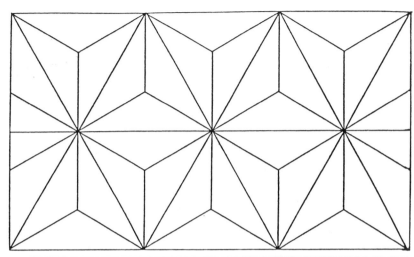

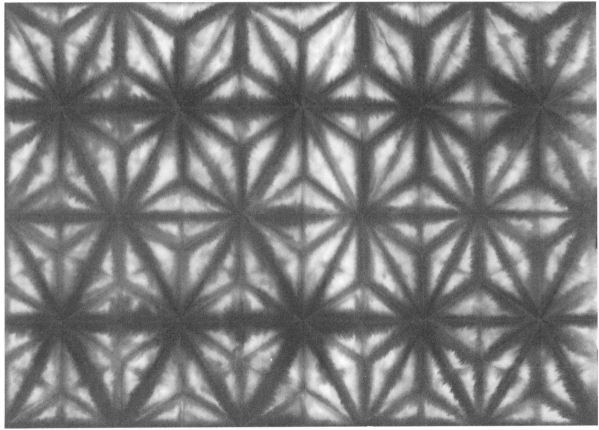

Triangles are all around us. Here is what the side of this basket would look like if it were enlarged. On the next page is what you might see when you look into a kaleidoscope.

Even if the triangles aren't the same shape, it is possible to cover a whole surface without any space in between. This patchwork pillow cover was made by sewing triangular pieces of cloth together.

When land is surveyed, it is measured by dividing a big
piece of land into lots of triangles.

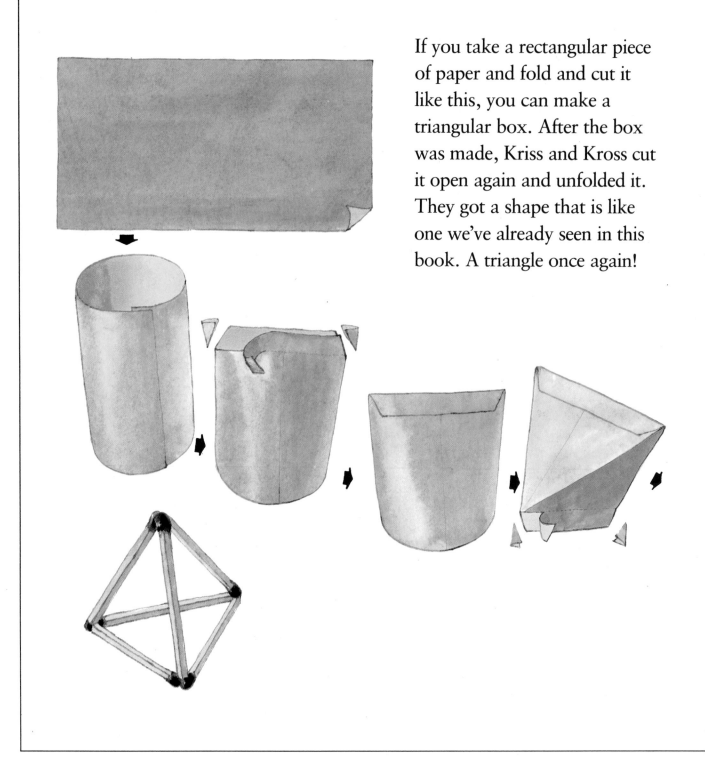

If you take a rectangular piece of paper and fold and cut it like this, you can make a triangular box. After the box was made, Kriss and Kross cut it open again and unfolded it. They got a shape that is like one we've already seen in this book. A triangle once again!

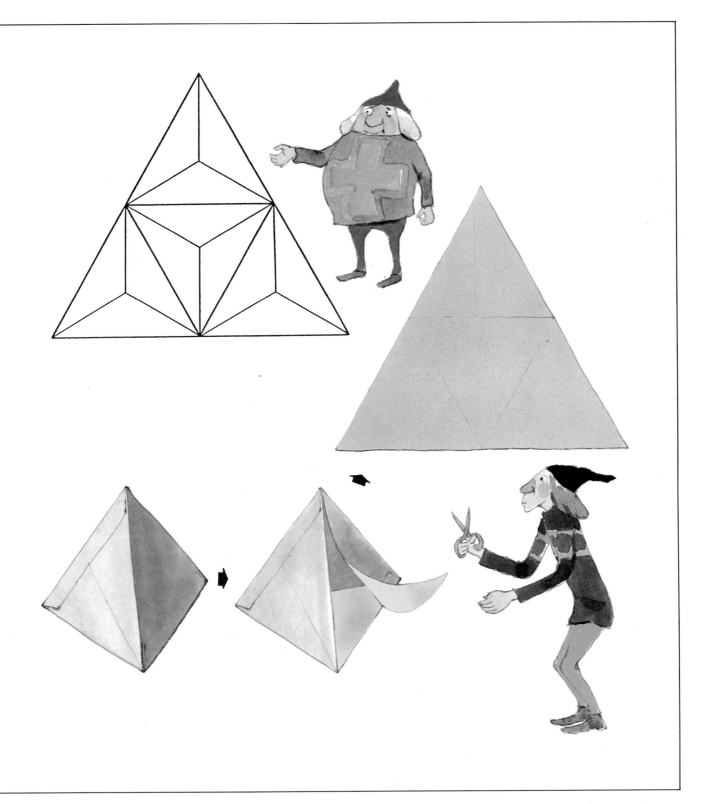

Here is another game.

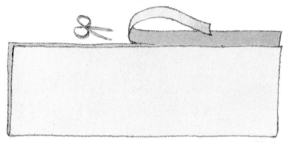

1. Fold a piece of drawing paper almost in half like this, and cut off a little bit. Then unfold the paper.

4. When you open it up, you can see the fold lines.

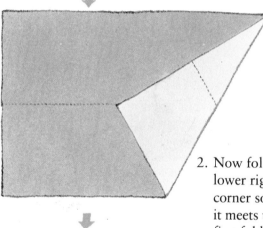

2. Now fold the lower right-hand corner so that it meets the first fold in the middle.

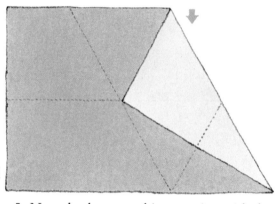

5. Now do the same thing starting with the upper right-hand corner.

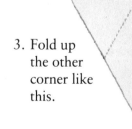

3. Fold up the other corner like this.

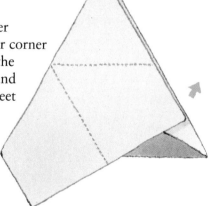

6. Fold over the other corner so that the right-hand edges meet neatly.

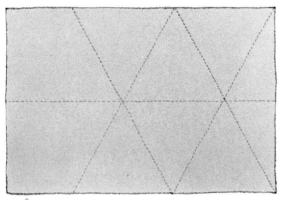

Fold several sheets
of paper this way
to make as many
as you wish!

7. Once again open it up so that you can see the fold lines.

8. Now, if you fold it like this,

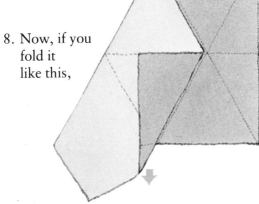

9. Unfold the paper and you get something like this.

10. Look at all the fold lines. By cutting along them, you can make all kinds of shapes. Triangles, diamonds, hexagons.

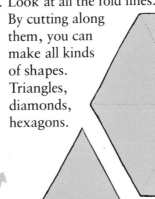

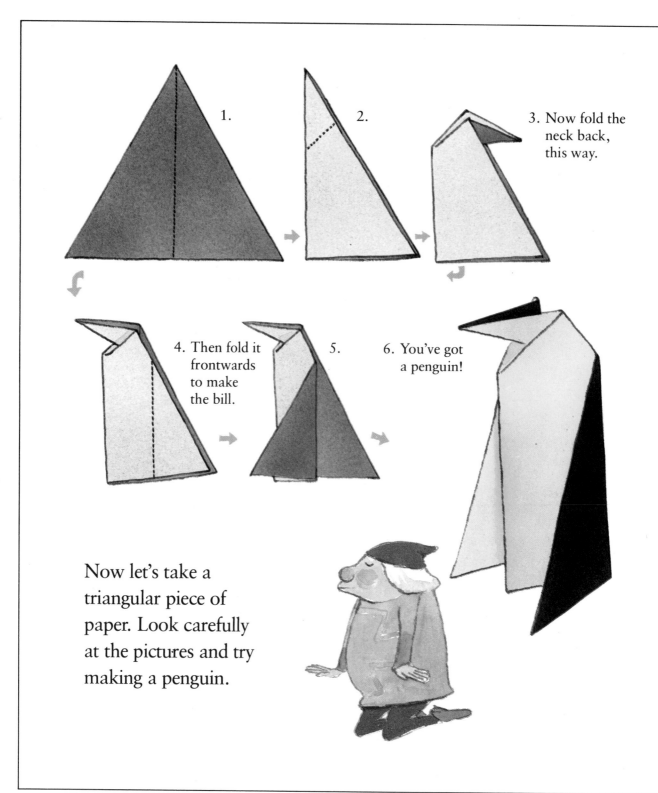

1.

2.

3. Now fold the neck back, this way.

4. Then fold it frontwards to make the bill.

5.

6. You've got a penguin!

Now let's take a triangular piece of paper. Look carefully at the pictures and try making a penguin.

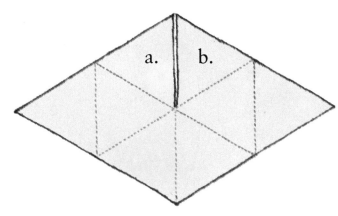

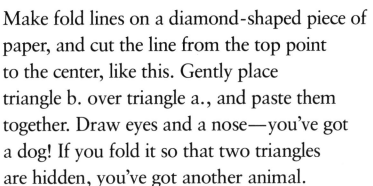

Make fold lines on a diamond-shaped piece of
paper, and cut the line from the top point
to the center, like this. Gently place
triangle b. over triangle a., and paste them
together. Draw eyes and a nose—you've got
a dog! If you fold it so that two triangles
are hidden, you've got another animal.
Is it a fox or a grumpy cat?

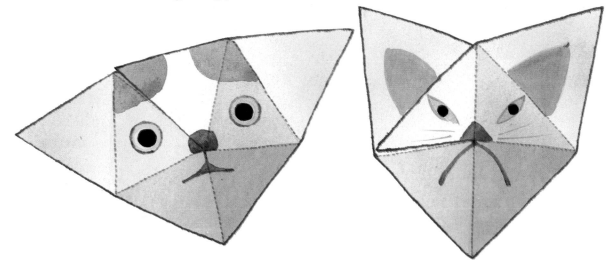

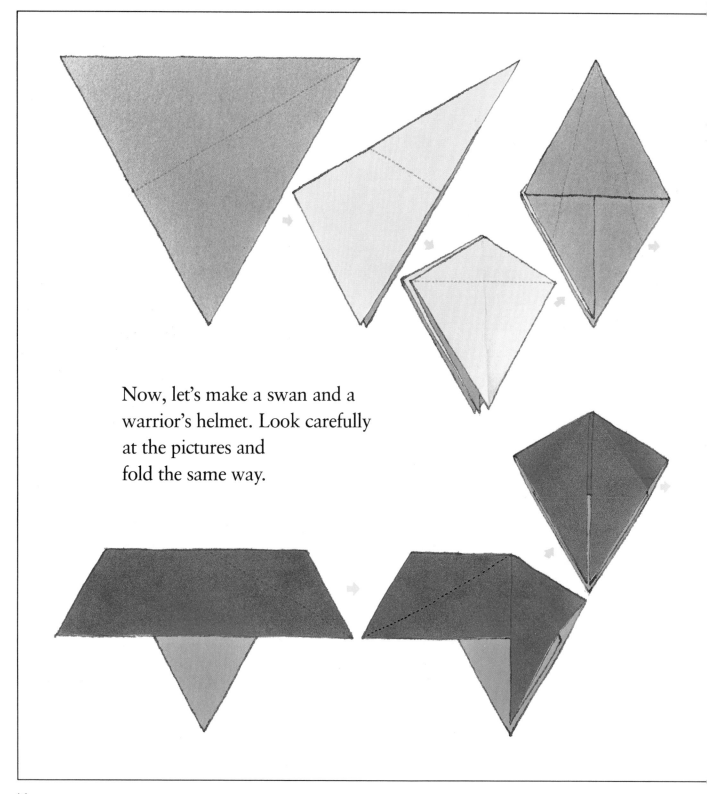

Now, let's make a swan and a
warrior's helmet. Look carefully
at the pictures and
fold the same way.

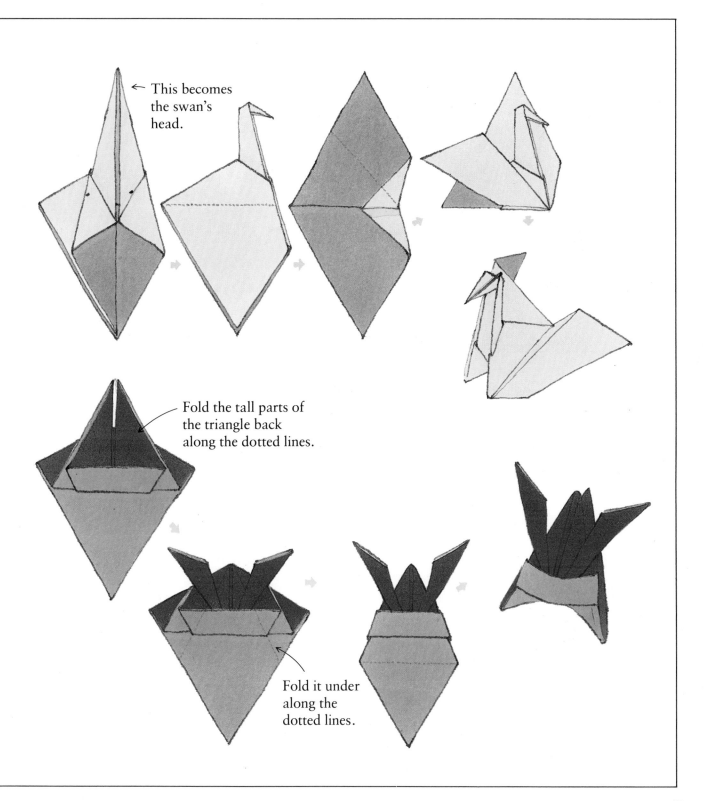

This becomes the swan's head.

Fold the tall parts of the triangle back along the dotted lines.

Fold it under along the dotted lines.

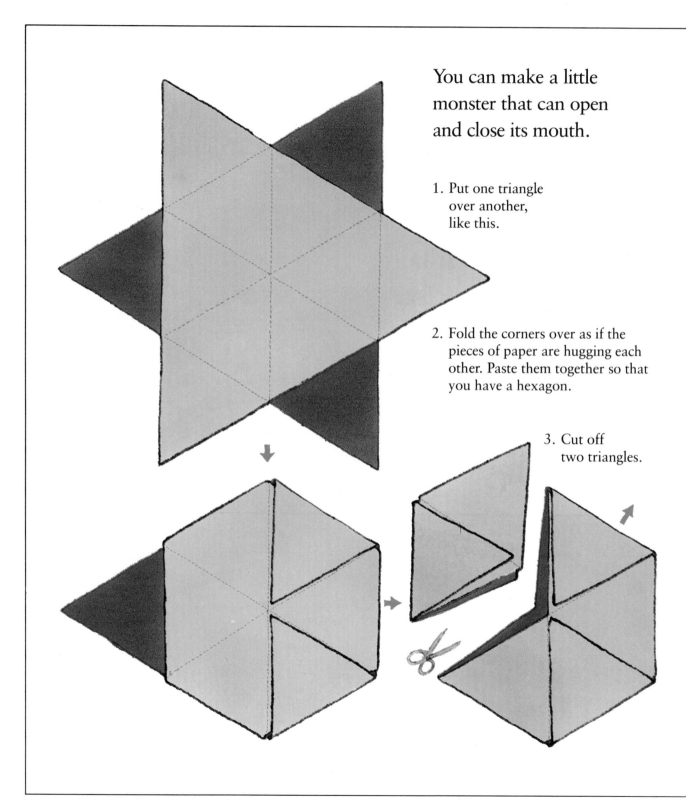

You can make a little
monster that can open
and close its mouth.

1. Put one triangle
   over another,
   like this.

2. Fold the corners over as if the
   pieces of paper are hugging each
   other. Paste them together so that
   you have a hexagon.

3. Cut off
   two triangles.

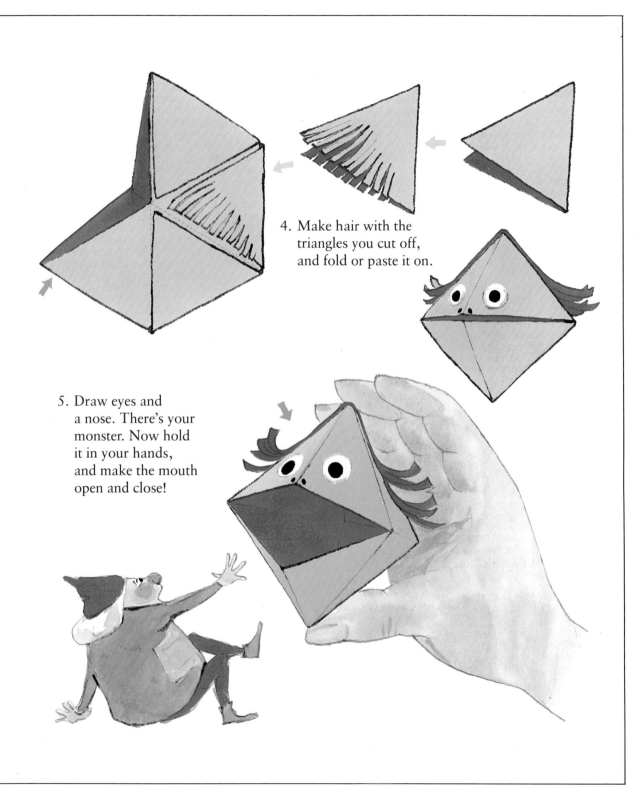

4. Make hair with the triangles you cut off, and fold or paste it on.

5. Draw eyes and a nose. There's your monster. Now hold it in your hands, and make the mouth open and close!

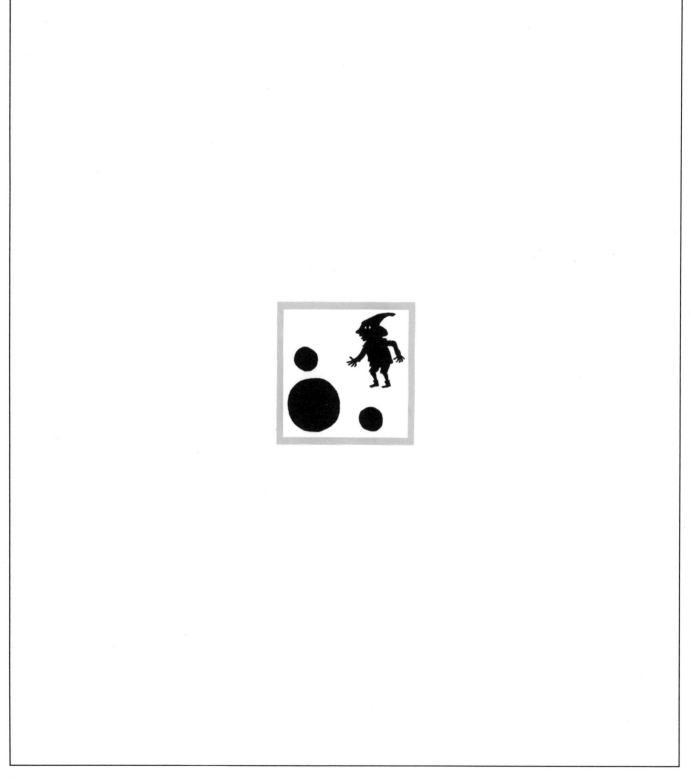

▪3▪

Mazes

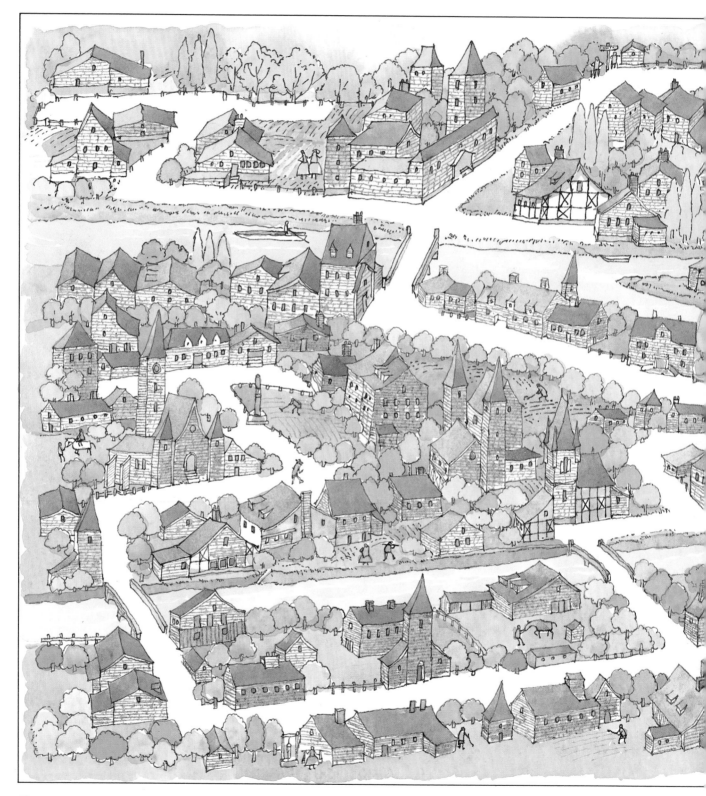

Kriss has a problem!
Which road should he take to get to the flag?

What's the best road for Kross to take to get all the way through the maze? With your finger, trace the road that Kross must take. Kriss has already found it.

In some mazes you must go back on the same path that you took to get in. Try it and see.

Take a good look at this
picture. The tree begins
with one stick. Then more
and more branches come out,
until there is a great big tree.
In other words, all of these
branches are joined to one
trunk. The tips of the branches
are not connected.

Our friends are making a maze by bending the branches of two trees.
Can you get from one tree to the other through the maze?

If you keep branching out from two lines, you can make
a pretty hard maze yourself! Try it on a friend.

How are the mazes on the left page

different from those on the right?

See if you can follow these two mazes with your finger.

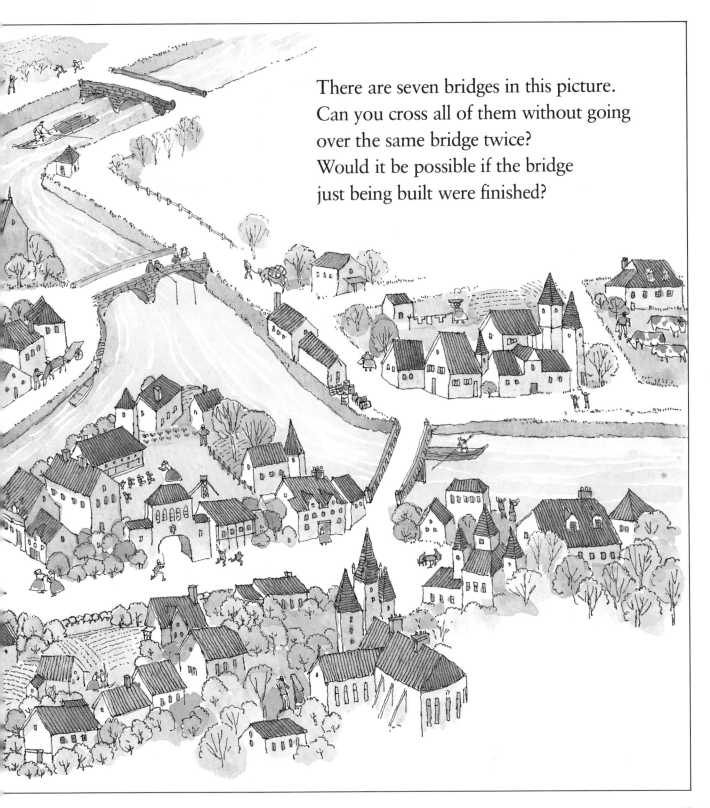

There are seven bridges in this picture.
Can you cross all of them without going
over the same bridge twice?
Would it be possible if the bridge
just being built were finished?

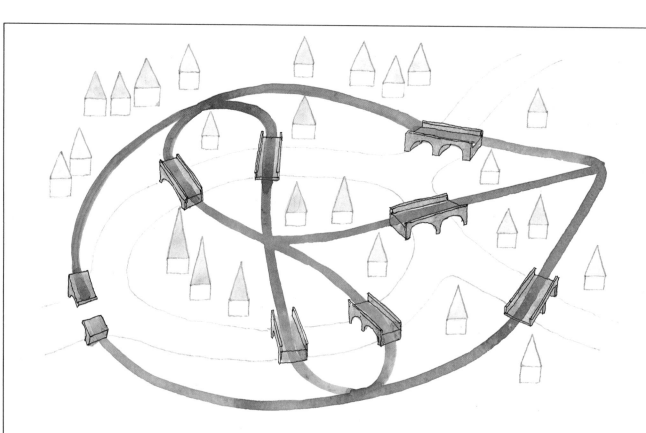

If we made the last page more simple,
this is what it would look like.
Trace the lines of the figures below,
but do not go over the same line twice.

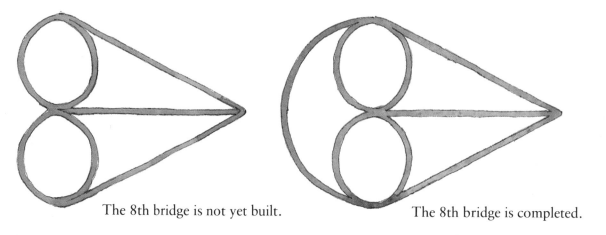

The 8th bridge is not yet built.

The 8th bridge is completed.

The game in this picture is made from one single piece of string.

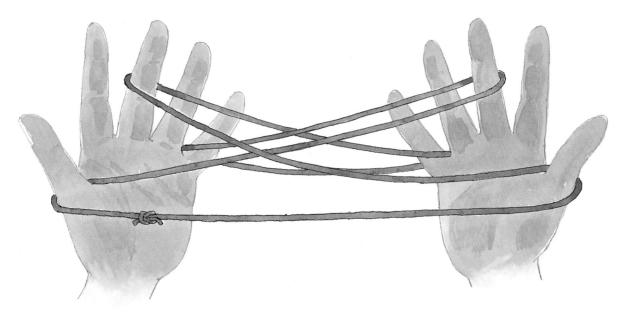

It is called a cat's cradle.
The shapes we form in a cat's cradle
can always be drawn
with just one line.

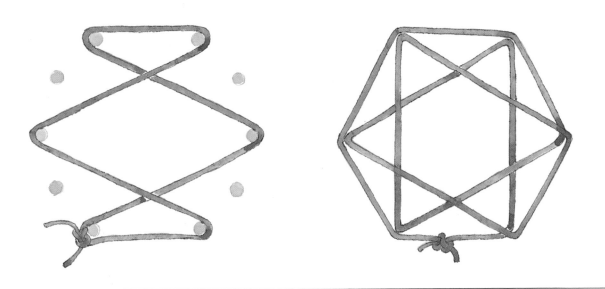

Some of these puzzles are made with one line.

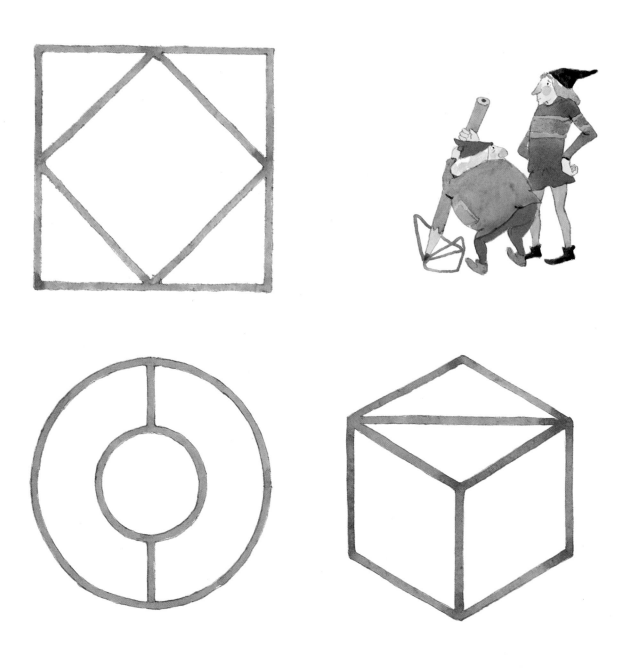

Trace them with your finger to see which ones they are.

This is made from just one cord.
It's based on a very, very old design.
Think about your sweater or a spider's web.
Each of them is a kind of
one-line design too, you know.

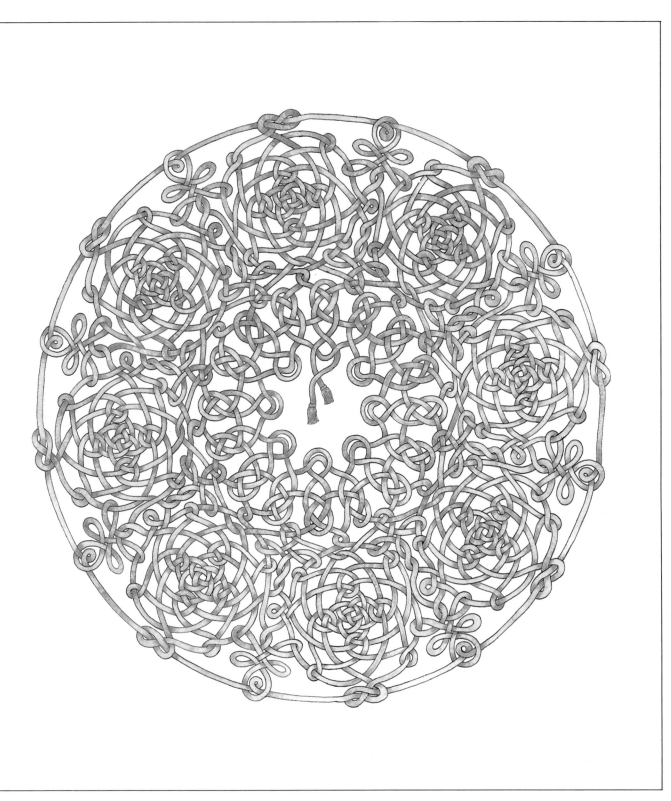

These mazes are on the walls of a very, very old temple in a far-away country.

The white part is the road. See if you can find
your way through with your finger.

▪ 4 ▪

Left and Right

Take a good look at the pictures on this page and compare them with the ones on the next page. They look the same, and yet something is different about them. What is it?

Now compare the pictures on these
two pages. What happens when you
put these pictures up to a mirror?

All of this comparing was so that you would
see that *left* and *right* are opposites.
Now put your own hand on top of this picture.

This is *left*.

Left and *right* look very much alike. But you can see that they are different, can't you?

This is *right*.

What things do you see on the *left* page?
And what is there on the *right* page?
How about the clock?
Is it on the *left* or the *right* page?

Every child is holding something.

What do they have in their *left* hands?
What is in their *right* hands?

"Raise your *right* hand." Everyone put up a
hand....Oops, but some children are wrong.
Which children put up the wrong hand?

The giraffe is on the *left* page and the tiger is on the *right*...right? What happens when you turn the book upside down?

Even though
something is on
the *right* when you
look at it, if somebody opposite
you looks at it, it will be
on that person's *left*.

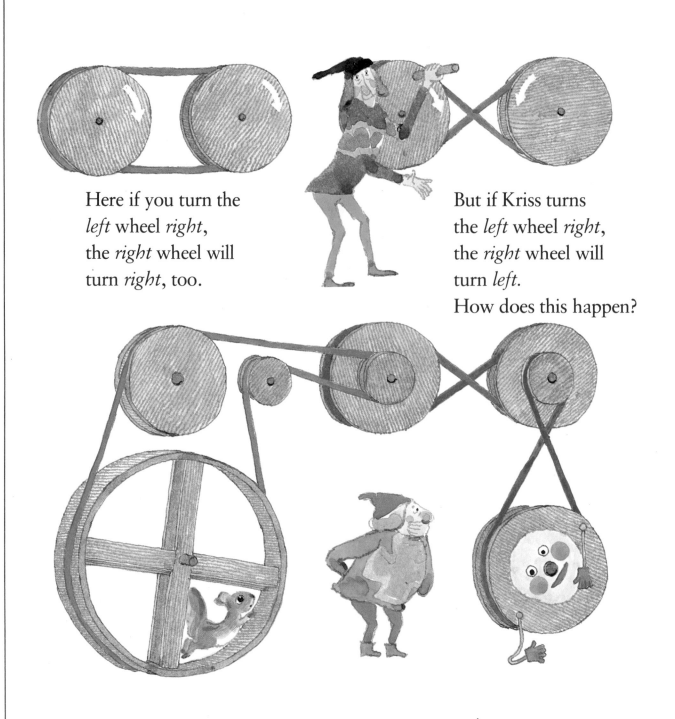

Here if you turn the *left* wheel *right*, the *right* wheel will turn *right*, too.

But if Kriss turns the *left* wheel *right*, the *right* wheel will turn *left*.

How does this happen?

How does
each of these
wheels turn?

Kross needs help. A girl guides him. "Go straight along this road, and you'll come to a gasoline stand. Turn *left* there and go straight, and you'll come to a telephone booth. Turn *left* again, and you'll come to a dairy farm."

"Go straight along this road..."

Can you explain to Kross how to get from the school
to the barber shop?

Zoo

Bank

"How do you get to the train station?" asks Kriss. "Well, let's see. You go straight along this road and..."

Help him get to the zoo, the restaurant, or the bank.

How do you get to the train station?
And the fire house?

Pretend that you want to walk someplace in this village.
Tell yourself how to get there.

Afterword

1 · Magic Liquid

Let's say that the stops made by a bus taking a circular route are labeled "A B C D E." A picture of this relationship can be made by drawing a circle and marking five points labeled "A B C D E" on it. When we make such a diagram, we completely ignore such factors as the distance between the stops, bends in the road, and the time it takes to get from one stop to another. We are considering only the position of the stops: A comes before B, and B before C.

It is not necessary to use a circle; a triangle, a square, or a much freer form would do just as well. All that is required is a closed outline, as we would get if we tied the ends of a piece of string together. No matter how the form of the outline changes, the correlation of position does not change. In short, we can see that under no circumstances will the order A B C D E become A C D E B.

If, in this way, we consider only the correlation of position, we can say that the figures on pages 22–25 are, from the viewpoint of position, all the same figure. This, in brief, is the concept behind the new field of math called topology.

Suppose we had a surface somewhat like a rubber handkerchief that we could stretch and shrink any way we liked. If we drew a person's face on this surface, and stretched and shrunk it however we pleased, we could see all kinds of fascinating changes. However, the correlation of position would remain the same.

Imagine that we could make an egg-shaped form from this rubber handkerchief. If we changed this form without any cutting or joining together, we could make a sugar cube form, or a pretzel; stretch it until it is long and thin and we could even tie it into a bow. However, no matter how hard we tried, we would not be able to make a form with a hole in it, such as a doughnut. At this point, we would conclude that an egg and a doughnut are physically different spatial figures. Topology pushes this concept further to study the endless possibilities of space and dimensions.

Topology got its start about 200 years ago with the theory of a Swiss mathematician, Euler. At that time, it was thought to be a strange sort of math, with no practical application. Today it may well be called the star of modern math.

The advances made in transportation and communication these days are rapidly changing our sense of distance, of what is far and near. For example, if you see someone off at the Tokyo airport, she may well have reached

Hong Kong by the time you drive back home. There are many examples of this sort without thinking about air travel. For instance, if a house is on the other side of a big river, without a bridge nearby, we would say that it is far, even though it is near as the crow flies. If we do not have diplomatic relations with a nearby country, it becomes a far-off land in our minds. But with the building of a bridge, the opening of a new road, or the normalization of diplomatic relations, the idea of distance changes completely.

2 · Exploring Triangles

Most adults know that in any triangle, the sum of the interior angles is equal to two right angles. I still remember marveling at how ingenious it was, when I learned this fact in my first geometry class back in junior high school.

We may well be filled with wonder that we can turn on the TV set with the push of a button or that we can talk to someone thousands of miles away on the phone; but such things were made by human beings for their own convenience. These achievements don't seem so marvelous when compared to the wonders of nature—how bees gather honey, or how birds migrate without losing their way.

It may not be easy to find triangles in nature, though by examining mineral crystals, examples of naturally formed triangles may be found. But if we consider the fields of civil engineering, architecture, transportation, and recreation, among others, we can search out hidden triangles everywhere.

Whether the triangles we are looking at have to do with measurement or with transportation, they have the same geometric properties as those we look at in the abstract.

For me, the mystery of why a red flower blooms is not nearly as wondrous as the ordered beauty of this silent form called a triangle. Triangles are a part of nature, but of a different order of nature than such things as birds and insects. Human beings are aware of this mystery, but even the cleverest person could not have created such a mystery.

This field of geometry based on triangles, constructed by Euclid more than 2,000 years ago, retains its beauty to this day. It is a model of easily demonstrated mathematical principles, and this is a field of knowledge which children will surely encounter in the future. It awaits as something inspiring, not for the sake of passing academic tests nor for the sake of becoming a civil engineer, but for the sake of its own coordinated beauty.

If I tried to explain the geometric concepts in this book, it would seem quite advanced, but it is easy to grasp if seen as a game. Unlike the formal study of geometry in which you move forward as you make proofs, children move forward in the book by playing, a much more enjoyable way to learn, as befits their ages.

There is an amusing story in which the great leader of Japan, Shogun Tokugawa Ieyasu,

when told in a lecture that the sum of the interior angles of a triangle is equal to two right angles, demanded, "Even if the triangle is as big as Lake Biwa [the biggest lake in Japan]?" Although one may laugh, it is true that in a triangle on a big spherical surface such as the earth, the sum of the interior angles is not necessarily equal to two right angles.

As we continue to study mathematics, we later see the birth of another aspect of geometry called "non-euclidean" geometry. But this revolution in knowledge could only have been gained by a creative approach that looked at triangles with inspired eyes.

3 ▪ Mazes

For a number of years I have been asking an acquaintance of mine in Moscow to send me a map of the city of Kaliningrad, but I was never able to get hold of one. Then to my amazement, I discovered a map of Königsberg in an old book of maps that I had. Königsberg, formerly a city in Prussia, is now the Soviet city of Kaliningrad. A happy discovery, for Königsberg/Kaliningrad is a model for the bridge problem contained in this book.

There are seven bridges in this city. The problem of whether one can cross all seven bridges and return to the starting point without retracing any steps was once supposed to be a favorite puzzle in this town. In one well-known story, Euler (1707–1783), a great Swiss mathematician) saw an important mathematical principle in this legendary tale and gave a mathematical explanation for it.

The explanation is as follows: Draw a diagram of the roads and bridges. Mark with points the places where the lines of travel cross.

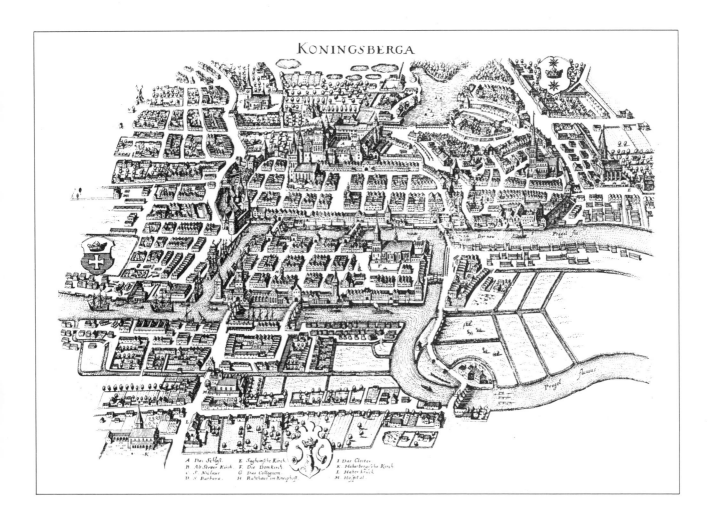

A Das Schloß.   E Saghensche Kirch.   I Das Closter.
B Ab Stewer Kirch.   F Die Domkirch.   K Haberbergische Kirch
C S. Niclaus   G Das Collegium   L Haber Kruck
D S. Barbara   H Rathhaus im Kneiphoff   M Hospital

If the number of lines (roads) gathered at a point is an even number, the point is called an even-number point; if the number of lines is odd, then it is called an odd-number point. If a diagram of a figure has more than three odd-number points, then it cannot be drawn (traveled) in one stroke, that is, without lifting the pencil or retracing steps.

To see if this is true or not, please try the one-stroke line problems in this book. Many people may feel that the one-line puzzles are too simple and childish to be thought of as mathematics. But consider for a moment the inside of a radio or a TV, both of which are complex mazes of lines. By using Euler's simple principle mentioned above, one can tell whether the electrical

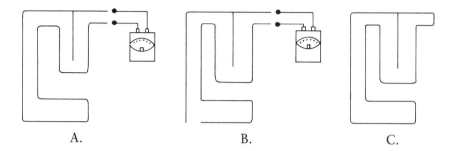

A.   B.   C.

current will flow or not.

Euler could not have imagined that this simple theory would be applied to the theory of electric circuits, or that it would lead to topology, the leading light among topics of modern math.

Speaking of circuits, do you know of an apparatus that tests circuits? Two wires, + (plus) and − (minus), come out of the tester. You connect these wires to an electric wire, and if the wire is intact, the current flows through; if the line is cut somewhere, the current doesn't flow.

The electric current flows through maze A, so we know that it is a closed circuit, like a dead-end maze with only one place to enter and exit. The tester makes it possible for us to know this without having to go inside the maze. In B we can pass through from the entrance to the exit, without retracing steps. If these circuits were mazes, the tester would tell us whether we could pass through them or not.

We can see that although figures A, B, and C appear to be the same maze, there are some important differences. Figure C differs from figures A and B, because we consider the space inside and outside of the figure rather than the lines or paths through it.

Mazes and continuous lines are different from one another, but in the field of phasial mathematics that has the high-sounding name of "circuit theory," they can be thought of as birds of a feather. Both range from very simple to very complex. But in the same way that the branches of a standing tree are understood to be joined to make one continuous unit, or as a string can be recognized as being in one piece, no matter how tangled, this distinction of whether a line or a path is connected or not, enables children to deal with mathematical principles at the most basic level. It is an idea that children need to grasp from their experience with puzzles such as these.

4 · Left and Right

I am thinking of an old friend of mine, who made a whirlybird out of bamboo, which flew so well that I begged. him to let me fly it. But

when I tried, it kept flipping out of my hand. No matter how hard I tried, I couldn't get it to work. But when my friend tried it, it would dance up into the air delightfully. I finally realized that he was left-handed. He had made the

position of the wings so that the bending of the wrist had to be done by a left-handed person.

I had another left-handed friend who had mastered the tonal range from the left. For him, the high notes had to be on the left of his instrument. So, he would play the harmonica upside down. This made me think that if he were to get a piano, it would have to be specially made, and since he would have to play the right-hand part with his left hand, and the left-hand part with his right hand, he would have to rewrite the musical score to allow him to do this.

When a motorcyclist is racing, the driver's body must lean into the curve, but if the motorcycle has a sidecar, the person sitting in the sidecar must stick most of his body out of the car while holding on, and just as in a yacht race, lean away from the curve to balance the centrifugal force. However, if you watch carefully, not all the sidecars do the same thing, even at the same curve. Some sidecars are attached on the left, and some on the right, and they have to adjust accordingly.

The problem of left-handedness and right-handedness often comes up in education. Most problems can be solved, but writing is designed for right-handed people, and being left-handed can be a disadvantage here.

Since I'm not a specialist, I don't know how

to deal with the problem, but I'll give it a try. Try practicing writing with the hand that you don't usually use. Since Romanized writing is from left to right, it would seem that being left-handed would be a particular disadvantage, but most left-handers write speedily with their left hand, and don't particularly have trouble learning to write. Parents need no longer be overly concerned about this.

Leonardo da Vinci, Babe Ruth, and the Japanese artist Ryuzaburo Umehara are some examples of famous left-handed people.

I looked up "right" in the dictionary. One of the many definitions said "toward the south if one is facing east." When I looked up "south," it said, "toward the right, if one is facing east." It is just that difficult to try to explain "right" in words. But if we draw it in a picture book, however, it is easier than explaining with words.

Left and right have meaning only in relation to the way one is facing. It's easy to make a mistake where the other person's situation is concerned, because viewpoint depends on the direction the person is facing. Teachers who wish to avoid confusion must often turn their back to the children to show that their right is the same side as the children's right, or must speak of right while pointing to their own left.

When the positional relation of left to right has been fully grasped, we can go on to the relation of direction: north, south, east, and west. The positional relation of the four directions is not self-centered, and since we can ask about position without worrying about which way others are facing, there are fewer mistakes. But unless there is common understanding of which way north is, the concept of the four directions is incomprehensible.

We speak of going up or going down in connection with transportation. Surveyors often speak of the ocean side or the mountain side. Such expressions of positional relation reach the ever more universal level of X and Y coordinates, and finally begin to seem like math.

When I traveled in Europe, I took a compass. When I lost my way, I compared the compass and the map to see where I was, but I soon realized that it didn't help, and gave it up after two or three tries.

It's fine on the sea or in the air where you can go in a straight line, but when driving on a road, the direction indicated by a compass is pretty near meaningless. The road bends every which-way, and we can't have a definite X axis and a Y axis as in coordinate geometry. For example, even if Paris is located to the north on the map, the road may often seem to be heading south.

In most of the world, where driving on the right side of the road is the rule, the exits of highways are usually on the right. Even if Paris is to the left of us, we exit to the right. And though we drive ever forward, the road makes a big arc, and eventually heads toward Paris.

LEFT AND RIGHT IN THE NATURAL WORLD by Martin Gardner is an excellent book which takes up the problem of left and right in an easy and interesting way. It is a good reference book for those of you who would like to know more about left and right.

MITSUMASA ANNO is known the world over for his highly original and thought-provoking picture books, and in 1984 he was awarded the Hans Christian Andersen Prize, the highest honor attainable in the field of children's book illustration. A man of many talents and interests, Mr. Anno shares his enthusiasm for art, nature, history, literature, mathematics, travel and people with young readers through his uniquely imaginative books. He feels that the mathematical laws that underlie nature are as beautiful as other aspects of the wonderful world we live in, and that even very small children can understand and appreciate them if they are clearly and appealingly presented. In this book, which offers very young children a learning experience that is as enjoyable as a game, he demonstrates his belief that mathematics is more than merely manipulating numbers, it is a way of thinking, and that it has bearing on all scholastic subjects, indeed on all forms of creative thought. Born in 1926 in Tsuwano, in Western Japan, Mr. Anno is a graduate of the Yamaguchi Teacher Training College and worked for some time as a teacher before becoming an artist. He now lives in Tokyo, but he travels all over the world to do research for his many books.

Other Books by Mitsumasa Anno
published by Philomel Books

Anno's Math Games

Anno's Math Games II

Anno's Britain

Anno's Faces

Anno's Counting House

Anno's Masks

Anno's All In A Day

Anno's Hat Tricks

Anno's U.S.A.

Anno's Italy

Socrates And The
Three Little Pigs

Anno's Journey

Anno's Mysterious Multiplying Jar

Anno's Sundial

Anno's Peekaboo

The publishers would like to thank Joan Oltman for her help in the translation
and preparation of this book.

Library of Congress Cataloging-in-Publication Data Anno. Mitsumasa,
1926—[Hajimete deau sūgaku no ehon. English] Anno's math games III/
by Mitsumasa Anno. p. cm. Translation of Hajimete deau
sūgaku no ehon. Summary: Picture puzzles, games, and simple
activities introduce the mathematical concepts of abstract
thinking, circuitry, geometry, and topology. ISBN 0-399-22274-X.
1. Mathematical recreations—Juvenile literature. [1. Mathematical
recreations. 2. Picture puzzles.] I. Title. II. Title: Anno's math
games 3. III. Title: Anno's math games three. QA95.A5613 1991
793.7′4—dc20   90-35398   CIP AC